Moving Mountains
Prayers for the Journey

By
Nathaniel L. Drysdale, M.Ed.

Copyright © 2012 Nathaniel L. Drysdale

All rights reserved.

ISBN: 0615667635
ISBN-13: 978-0615667638
NLD Publishing

DEDICATION

This is book is dedicated to my wife, our children, my praying grandmother and the rest of our family for their love & support along with many thanks to friends around the globe.

May God's peace be your guide and Christ's love be your strength. Never quit praying because God never stops listening.

CONTENTS

THE JOURNEY 1

THE MOUNTAIN 4

    REFLECTION I 10

THE BASE 11

    REFLECTION II 15

THE FACE 16

    REFLECTION III 20

THE CRAG 21

    REFLECTION IV 25

THE COL 26

    REFLECTION V 31

THE TREELINE 32

    REFLECTION VI 38

THE SNOWLINE 39

    REFLECTION VII 45

THE PEAK 46

    REFLECTION VIII 51

MOUNTAINS MOVED 52

THE JOURNEY

Often times in our lives we are faced with challenges, situations, and plain old problems. We know about prayer. We think we know about God. We think we have this life all in control. Then, amazingly life just has a way of falling to bits and pieces around us. That is what this is about. The falling to pieces but more importantly the putting them back together.

My prayer's sometimes may have seemed simple, some really deep and some well they were just there. The prevailing theme is that these prayers got me through some of my most challenging times. Now, I am not going to get all religious and act like I really always wanted to pray and there were many days I skipped praying altogether. Yet, I am glad that God never skipped out on me on those rough days.

It is in the roughest times that we find the greatest gems. Think about it…if you never had a trying time you would never know how good some friends were to stick by and how bad others truly are. You would never suspect certain people to have stood by you. You would never know you could make it through a situation. You would never know how wonderful you really are.

If we are going to move mountains in our lives then we have to be mountain movers. One of the great things about a mountain climber is that they celebrate the times they made it to the top of the mountain as well as the times they almost did not because in each was an opportunity to learn. Because life is not about the winning and losing rather it is about the Journey to get there.

Throughout this collection I hope you find a prayer that can lift you up and help you to move your mountains. Sometimes in the midst of moving your biggest obstacles and mountains in life, God swoops, down, and plugs a thought in your head. Consider these prayers those thoughts. Hmm, I feel a thought coming on right now.

So let us now begin our mountain moving journey…

PRAYERS FOR THE JOURNEY

THE MOUNTAIN

1. a natural structure like a very big hill that is much higher than the usual level of land around it
2. a large mass of something resembling this, as in shape or size.

Dear Father,

In this world we are constantly seeking Lord, seeking the right job, right things, the right place of worship, the right relationships, yet how often do we ask you about the things we seek beforehand. Lord your word said "seek and we shall find... knock and it will be opened". Father we know this is true. Lord we pray that we seek and knock and ask for things in you. Lord, let us recognize you are the giver and supplier of all our needs. Today father we pray that we will know and understand that if we put you first all the other things will fall into place. We bless your name and your face we will seek.

Amen.

Dear Father,

Today be our strength and order our steps. Let us see that the steps to victory start with you and end with You. Let us know that we do not walk alone. You are with us in every trial, adversity, conflict and in the good times of happiness, promotion and blessings. You will redeem and You Lord will protect. Bless each of us here with Your abundance and with Your strength. We will praise Your name forever and help us to follow the pathway that is ordered by You.

Amen.

Dear Lord,

Let the fruits that we produce show that we are part of your tree. Lord, let us not be hypocrites in the kingdom but let us live righteously in your sight. We pray that you will remove every stumbling block and obstacle within our path. Break the bounds that tie us down to a life of mediocrity so that we can soar like the Eagle in on earth as it is being done in heaven. Let your will be done in everything and your power take control and we will be careful to give you the glory, honor and praise.

Amen.

Dear God,

We love and praise you for the trinity and for your triumphant love that we could not ever surpass. We thank you for making provisions and ways out no way for us. We thank you for doors opening and areas closing that needed to be closed. We thank you that we are aware that through all of these things you prove to us that you are the only true God and your son Jesus Christ. We thank you for being real to us.

Amen.

Dear Father,

We love you for your promise to constantly take care of us. We bless and honor your name as supreme king. Thank you for giving us peace. Let us understand that according to your scriptures we will have tribulation (problems, issues, discontent) but you have overcome the world. So that we can in the midst of worldly chaos still have an everlasting and comforting peace. You are awesome and we honor you. In Jesus name we all say....

Amen.

Dear Father in heaven,

What a wonderful assurance your son has given us on this day and we thank you for the blessing. The word says "I pray not thou should take them out of the world." Meaning Lord you have a plan and purpose for us here on earth. Here in our neighborhoods, here in our families and work environments but more important is the following portion of the verse "...but that thou should keep them from evil." Your son prayed that since he doesn't want us to be taken out from the world that you would cover us with your protect and keep evil away from us. Lord we thank you today for the blessing of protection. No matter what storm or adversity may come in our path, your son Jesus already prayed for us in advance. May your grace and love ever flow for thy word is truly the truth.

Amen.

REFLECTION I

For your blessings
We seek
For your love
We yearn
For your covering
We pray
For your care
We say
Thanks!

THE BASE

1. *the bottom support of anything; that on which a thing stands or rests: a metal base for the table.*
2. *a fundamental principle or groundwork; foundation; basis: the base of needed reforms.*

Dear Father,

We thank you for your words. We thank you for the power that is in what you say. We thank you that your word does what it is set out to do. Father, let us prosper in what your word says. Just as the rain waters the earth to make it bring forth flowers and food for us to eat; So let the rain of your spirit water our hearts and lives that we too can bring forth fruit of the harvest in terms of tithes and offerings. Let us be blessed to be a blessing in Jesus name.

Amen.

Dear Lord,

We thank you for your overshadowing blessings in our lives. Lord, how wonderful and glorious it is to know that you have a covenant of peace and kindness to keep us safe. Lord we thank you for the fact that you make us lie down in green pastures and you lead us beside still waters in this our very busy life. Lord we thank you for your mercy and your ever present grace. Oh how we love you and ask you to continue blessing us this day and in the days to come in Christ's name!

Amen.

Dear Jesus,

We are grateful today because we know that you live. How awesome it is to know that we serve a risen savior. It is more than just rising from the grave but it is rising from the depths of our hearts and souls to the lives that we choose to have on this earth. Lord, let us know that since we joined your fold we will now also live forever, if not in this life then, in the life to come with you. You live so that we might live. Father we pray that on this day we will live to your expectations for us in Jesus name.

Amen.

Dear Lord,

We pray and give thee thanks lord. We thank you for your spirit Lord. Help us to let your spirit allow us to be a witness and effective to helping the world rather than tearing it down with condemnation. Teach us discernment and show us how to open up the prisons that have so many lives captive. Teach us to be speakers of good tidings because so many in the world speak evil and ill words. Above all teach us to be kind one to another. This we pray in Jesus name.

Amen.

REFLECTION II

Teach our inner spirit

What it needs to know

So that daily as people

We can learn, live and

Grow!

THE FACE

*1. a side of a mountain or building
that is high and very steep*

Dear Father,

What a wonderful blessing to know that you have our prayers covered. If we pray believing that we receive then we SHALL have. We love the confidence we have that as your children you will hear and answer our prayers. It does not matter if our prayers are for financial blessings, medical blessings, spiritual blessings or general blessings for ourselves and our families. We are blessed. Yet, we are careful to understand that we need to forgive one another even as you forgive us. So Lord, in asking for blessings we also ask forgiveness so when we stand before you we are blameless and ready for what you blessed us to receive.

Amen.

Dear Father in heaven,

We love you. We worship you. We thank you. Father it is a blessing to know that you sent your son Christ for our sake that we can become new creatures. Christ came that we could have a chance to commune once again with you. In all of our old actions, our sinful nature, our dark pasts that may have been tainted with shame and broken promises, yet, now we are new so we grateful. We say thank you father for a second chance. Thank you for a renewed life. Thank you for the fact that every promise you give is sure. Thank you again for your son.

Amen.

Dear Jesus,

We thank you today for your mercy and your grace and your love. We praise you for your sacrifice. Master, father, friend we thank you for giving us a promise of a new spirit and a new heart. Removing the stone of all our hurts and pains from past relationships, family matters, untimely concerns and destructive friendships. We thank you for replacing it with flesh of love and understanding and warmth that we may walk with you and in your statues. Thank you on this day for rejuvenation so that we can live onward and upward to your glory.

Amen.

Dear God,

In a world faced with such calamity and distress we know that we have a protection that surpasses all understanding. We have seen earthquakes, floods, hurricanes, typhoons, and Mt. St. Helens is on the edge of eruption. We are witnessing strife, political unrest and health issues of all sorts and type. We have been through trials, persecutions and tribulations. Yet, in still through all this we can say "No weapon formed against us shall prosper". Father your love is amazing that even in the midst of all the adversities we face and have faced in the past we still come out on top. Why, because father we know that this is our heritage and we praise your name for that. Father, bless us this day. Watch over every situation and be our guide for every concern.

Amen!

REFLECTION III

In our distresses
You hear our cries
In our tears
You wipe our eyes
In our loneliness
You are our friend
You are ever there
Until the end

THE CRAG

1. a very steep rough part of a cliff or mountain

Dear Father,

Thank you for being our king and lord. When we give our lives to you we know that we are kept in your hands. So why do we question? Why do we get tempted to do wrong? For as your word says, "What profit is it to gain the world and lose our soul." Father helps us to keep our motives in check so that we are doing what is in your heart for us to do. Father let us be good stewards, resources, and governors over the body and soul you have given us to do your will. In Jesus name we pray.

Amen.

Dear Father,

Thank you for love and your glory. Thank you for your word. We know that you will come quickly. Father you are just an awesome God and we will take care that no one steals our crown. Many of us have been through problems and situations that threaten us to forget who we are in your kingdom. Lord let us walk in this earth knowing that our salvation is sure and we are a royal priesthood and a chosen generation. Let us walk as sons and daughters of a heavenly father in Jesus name.

Amen.

Dear Father in heaven,

We come to you today with outstretched arms and hands seeking to reverence your name and praise just for who you are. Father let us not find ourselves tied down by burdens and weaknesses. Father let us not get roped in by insecurities to the sense that we constantly need a sign for your miracles. Let us instead rise up to your standards and be what you want us to be. Let us live a life of knowing we are the works of God. We can live this life and do the works of God only when we know and understand that we are the perfect work of him that loves us. We bless and praise and thank you for your son.

Amen.

Dear Father,

Lord we bless your name cause you are always there. At times in periods of our life we may feel like we have been abandoned or that we are walking this journey all alone. But, we know through your words that you will never leave us nor forsake us. Father, help us to be calm in the midst of chaos no matter what comes our way. Even when we face difficult decisions in our lives for we know you will be with us through it all. We love adore and worship you...

Amen.

REFLECTION IV

You are the movements
In our hearts
You are the voice
That guides our paths
You are the hope
That we pray for
You are the light
In our way
You are the prayer
In the morning
You are our praise
In the evening
You are all
That we need
And for that we say
Thank you!

THE COL

1. *the lowest point of a ridge connecting two mountain peaks, often constituting a pass*

Dear Lord,

On this day rejoice. We give thanks to your name because you are good. Lord no matter what roadblocks or stumbling blocks we may face we will not be moved for you have not given us the spirit of fear. Instead God, in you we have power and strength and a sound mind; which we can use to defeat the enemy, conquer hurts with love and have focused clear thoughts on your will and way. We thank you for your mercy and giving us clarity this day.

Amen.

Dear Lord,

Today let us rejoice in the treasure of your word. How it touches our lives and makes us whole and complete. We honor the fact that you allow us to freely partake and read. Some many religions do not give easy access to what their teachings are but we know that we serve the true and only God. Daily, weekly, even secondly we can open the bible and let the words soak into our souls to melt our hearts and steer us in the pathway of righteousness. Father, we adore you this day for the access we have in your kingdom.

Amen.

Dear Lord,

How sweet it is to know that all things work out for good for your children that love you. Father your word did not say some things; it did not say one thing, rather Lord it said all things work together for good. Father, we love and adore you knowing that no matter what we are facing and battles we are going through uphill; we know we serve an "all things" God that is working in the background of our lives. Lord, let us reflect back this day and see the good that came from situations we thought were bad. In Christ's name we pray.

Amen.

Dear Lord,

Today we pray that you will bless us greatly that we can live according to your word and fear you that made heaven and earth. Not a fear of evil lord but rather a fear of love and respect and awe for the awesomeness of you. Lord, we reverence you and will give you all the praise and honor due to your name. We love You with all our heart and mind and soul. Lord this day help us to walk and think and talk the wisdom and words you pour into us and above all— Lord whatever is going on in our lives let your love reign that we may walk in peace in Jesus name we pray.

Amen.

Dear Jesus,

Allow us to lives that are becoming of you of Lord. Let us not relish in the cares of this world. Lord we pray that even as you bless daily, monthly, weekly, that you allow us to always remember it is all because of you. Lord help us to be humble knowing that nothing in this world can we do on our own. It is in you oh Lord, that we move and live and have our being. Master we reverence your name and understand that you alone are sovereign and have full control. Bless us this day in all that we do.

Amen.

REFLECTION V

Humility is what we long for
Guidance is what we need
Your presence is what revives us
And your love
Is what makes every day worth living for!

THE TREELINE

1. the zone, at high altitudes or high latitudes, beyond which no trees grow.

Dear Father,

We love the wonderful guide book you have given us called the Bible because as the verse in Revelation above states ...we will overcome and have power over the nations. Lord help us not to forget that no matter what we are facing and going through illness, death, strife in the workplace, added responsibilities, parenting, or guiding. Let us know that if we overcome then we win! Father, the race is not for the swift but for those that endure to the end. So let us endure through all we may face this day that at the end we will be the heads and not the tails. In Jesus name

Amen!

Dear Father,

Lord we bless thee today for allowing the Holy Spirit to come and dwell amongst us in this crazy world. We thank you for the fruit of the spirit of love, and joy and self-control and the others. Father, we thank you that as Christians we can have peace in the midst of war, kindness in the midst of rage, Love in the midst of hatred and joy in the midst of unquestionable pain. Father that is what makes the Christian journey so unique is that You, Lord, settle our emotions. Father on this day let us exercise the fruit of the spirit you have given us that we can walk uprightly and be a witness for you in Christ's name.

Amen!

Dear Father,

It continues to amaze us how simple and plain your word can be. Even though the Bible was composed hundreds of years ago everyday it is still relevant to our situations in life. Father for this we praise you. Lord, help us be mindful of what goes out of our mouths. Let us not use your name in vain. Let our mouths be filled with blessings and not curses. Father, we praise you that our words have power so we should be careful what we say. On this day no matter how upset or angry or disappointed we may get allow us to fill our mouths with words of encouragement so we can be a witness for someone else to see.

Amen.

Dear Father,

We praise you Lord because you are awesome. We worship you because you alone wonderful and unique. Lord no matter what comes into our path you are the strength of our life, so we have no fear. Lord we will not fear the economy, we will not fear who becomes president, we not fear our bills, our responsibilities, nor will we have fear of relationships. Lord, you are our salvation and we will bless you for that continuously.

Amen.

Dear Jesus,

Lord we love you. You are the Messiah, the chosen one, the lily of all our valleys'. How we worship you for your love. Many of us know our parents love us, our husbands and wives love us and our friends love us. Yet, still how many of them have so much loved that they would voluntarily die for us? How many would trade themselves to be tortured instead of us. How many would walk down the path for us knowing most of us, do not listen. We do not follow your path perfectly; we fall short so many times. Yet Lord you knew this would happen; you knew we would not love you for most of our lives as you loved us and you still made a way. We give you praise Lord and we want to say today...

WE LOVE YOU...BACK!

Dear Father,

We thank you because you are a forgiving and wonderful God. Your wrath has been spared from us because of your tenacious love that you have for us. Father, yes it is true, that we make mistakes and cause problems and strife. However, Lord you know it and see it and still forgive us anyhow. Lord today we pray to be more like you and learn to forgive and forget. Forgive the hurts, forget the pain but remember the lesson. Father, teach us, guide us and mold us in Jesus name.

Amen.

REFLECTION VI

You are our teacher when things are dark
You show us the ways that we should walk
Sometimes it seems scary and the path dimly lit
It is then you hold our hands
So we can go over it.
Thank you for showing us with kindness and care
For being there when we stumble
And when we are unaware
Always be our teacher and our guide.
And from your face oh Lord.
We shall never hide.

THE SNOWLINE

1. *the line, as on mountains, above which there is perpetual snow.*

Dear Father,

We love you and adore you. We thank you for all that you have done. You are wonderful and amazing. Father, teach us your will through the word. Father, helps us be a living sacrifice one that is worthy of your love and care that you freely give to us each day. Help us to present our bodies to you holy, blameless, most of all acceptable. Lord, allows us to be a witness for you each and every day not just from our lips but more so from the lives that we live.

Amen.

Dear Lord,

You are a mighty God this day and we praise you for your mercy. We ask that you continue to bless us and keep us from evil. Lord we will always pray so that when evil comes, we can find refuge in you and escape. Father, teach us, watch us, hold us, and protect us from life's evil. So we can one day stand before your throne and enter into the kingdom of heaven.

Amen.

Dear Father,

Lord you are our father of mercy and life. We worship you daily and thank you for your care. Lord how excellent is your name today. We thank you that we can call on you when we need you. You never get to weary to listen to our cry. How wonderful to know our Savior hears our voice and in return we know that you will save us. Keep us in your care every day. We adore you this day.

Amen.

Father,

We come before your throne with expectant hearts. We understand how great and sovereign you are in our life and we thank you for knowing all things about us. Today we rejoice in your word and presence because you are good. we seek after your righteousness and ask for your blessings. Allow us to ask and knock and seek out that which is good in your kingdom. Help us to reach out and better control our environments and let us know that in your word and your will all things are truly possible. Lord, we will keep knocking and seeking till the doors are opened.

Amen.

Our Father in Heaven,

We come before you today to honor you for who you are. Lord, how excellent is your name. How wonderful and victorious you are. Lord to day we are reminded that whatever comes in our paths that you are more than able to turn sorrows into joy. Weeping may endure for a night but we know that joy comes in the morning. So what let us take this day as a new opportunity instead of trials, let us have triumphs. Let us make good use of the day you have presented to us.

Amen.

Dear Father,

Today we celebrate peace. Father even in this time of elections and old government and new government enactments; we can still celebrate the peace we have in you. Father, we know that no matter what government, systems, policies and people are in place in our lives, at work, or home: that we will have tribulation. Yet, we also know that you gave us the strength to overcome all no matter what may take place. we are more than victorious through you.

May the God of peace, be with us all.

Amen.

REFLECTION VII

It is better to value your Life and relationship with God, than to value the cars in the driveway or dollars in the bank.

Why…?

Because the cars in the driveway depreciate and rust…the dollars in the bank are only as stable as the government it is written against.

But your worth increases every day by the lives you come in contact with, the smile you send across the hall and wisdom that comes from every triumph and mistake.

THE PEAK

1. the pointed top of a mountain or ridge.
2. the highest or most important point or level.
3. the maximum point, degree, or volume of anything

Dear God,

Today we come before you saying thank you for being in control of our lives. We thank you for allowing the good and the bad to happen so we might learn responsibility. Teach us to be faithful stewards of your word and your will. Teach us to watch our finances, our friendships, or service to others and our service to our jobs. So that one day you will say, "Job well done" to us and we can celebrate with you. Father we know it is hard sometimes yet we also know you have made the provisions.
This we pray!

Amen.

Dear Father,

Lord, we want to give you thanks and glory today for all you have done and are doing. Father we love you and worship you and ask that you keep us in your care. Father, teach us to value ourselves and protect our souls that you have given us. Let us not be complacent and ended falling short when we stand before your throne. Let us live everyday as how you would have us to live.

Amen.

Father,

We bless your name and are thankful for the wonderful works you have made. Father, today as the scriptures say Lord we pray for you to strengthen and to keep evil and unbelief out of our hearts. Let us keep a watchful eye on each other so that we can grow in faith together and keep our hearts softened to be molded by your word. we know how cunning evil is to deceive us in sin, yet if we look after our brothers and sisters perhaps Lord you will enable us to see the snares others do not see. May this day we make a commitment to be our brothers' and sisters' keepers in Jesus name.

Amen.

Father,

We thank you for today because you are the mighty conqueror in battle. Lord we lift your name up. Father helps us every day to maintain this love that you so freely gave to us that we might not sin against thee. Father, teach us to love the good and bad circumstances for they are all stepping stones to victory. Father, let us love you so much that in turn we abhor evil for fear of hurting you, and disappointing you. For if we love in this super natural way, in your word it states we will have victory and overcome the world.

Amen.

Dear Father,

It is amazing how much the world is always trying to get ahead. We try to overcome death with medical miracles. We try to overcome our frustrations with pills. We try overcome poor social skills with matching services. And, Lord we even try to overcome salvation and your convictions, with spiritualism and entertainment. Yet, the bible clearly states that the saints overcame the devil with something so precious and yet so, free...their testimony and the blood of the lamb. Teach us to testify. Teach us to tell of your goodness where ever we go. Lord, even so as we move beyond that teach us something even more important and that is to love you more than our very own lives. Because although they testified and had your powerful blood on their lives they also loved not their lives so you were able to take control and make them overcomers. Today if any of us are struggling. Let us testify of God's goodness in-spite of the situation.

Amen.

REFLECTION VIII

"…In the last days, the mountain of the LORD's house
will be the highest of all—
the most important place on earth.

It will be raised above the other hills,
and people from all over the world will stream there to worship.
People from many nations will come and say,
"Come, let us go up to the mountain of the LORD,
to the house of Jacob's God.
There he will teach us his ways,
and we will walk in his paths."
For the LORD's teaching will go out from Zion…"
—Isaiah 2:1-3

MOUNTAINS MOVED

We never know when we might be faced with obstacles or times when our hearts are truly sorry for course of events or things. Sometimes a thought runs through your mind that simply says "Oh God I need help!" Sometimes it is more than that. It is the times when we lay in bed or on a couch wondering how we got into the predicament that we find ourselves in. It is the times when tears are flowing down our cheeks. It is the times when our eyes are puffy and we do not want others to know that they are full and about to burst into tears.

It's when men in a look of solidarity with hardened lines on their faces brush off the pain and bury it deep within their spirits. These are what the prayers are made of. These are what makes us resilient and what makes me know that there must be a God somewhere.

Why? Because if we can feel so much pains at times and hurts—then there has to be an opposite. There has to be "Someone" out there that knows our hurts and our pains and understands the times we are down or depressed.

When I pray, I feel something that I hope you feel as well. Regardless of religion, customs or creed I hope you feel the hope that can be found in the midst of the pain. I hope you can feel the sense of inner peace knowing you have taken your pains and placed them in the hands of something higher than yourself. You have lifted them before God—as the Hebrews would say "The God of Abraham, Isaac, and Jacob". We cannot go through this world alone. Although, you and I may try to and feel it will all workout. Although, we like to think this is all there is to living. I hope that through these prayers you may have seen that it is more than that.

So let's pray together often. Anytime you feel the need pick up a prose and read it with sincerity. I am already in agreement with you on two things:
1. God knows your heart when you pray whether you are new to praying or a seasoned veteran of asking and listening for help.
2. There is no situation that is too big, too hard, and too tough for God to do.

Praying always to have mountains moved!

www.ingramcontent.com/pod-product-compliance
Lightning Source LLC
LaVergne TN
LVHW051210080426
835512LV00019B/3189